TEAMWORKS
WORKING TOGETHER WORKS

Compiled by Dan Zadra and Kristel Wills
Designed by Steve Potter and Jenica Wilkie

COMPENDIUM™
PUBLISHING

live inspired.

ACKNOWLEDGEMENTS

These quotations were gathered lovingly but unscientifically over several years and/ or contributed by many friends or acquaintances. Some arrived—and survived in our files—on scraps of paper and may therefore be imperfectly worded or attributed. To the authors, contributors and original sources, our thanks, and where appropriate, our apologies. —The Editors

WITH SPECIAL THANKS TO

Jason Aldrich, Gerry Baird, Jay Baird, Neil Beaton, Josie Bissett, Jan Catey, Doug Cruickshank, Jim Darragh, Jennifer & Matt Ellison, Rob Estes, Michael Flynn & Family, Shannan Frisbie, Jennifer Hurwitz, Heidi Jones, Cristal & Brad Olberg, Janet Potter & Family, Diane Roger, Jenica Wilkie, Clarie Yam & Erik Lee, Kobi, Heidi & Shale Yamada, Justi, Tote & Caden Yamada, Robert & Val Yamada, Kaz, Kristin, Kyle & Kendyl Yamada, Tai & Joy Yamada, Anne Zadra, August & Arline Zadra.

CREDITS

Compiled by Dan Zadra and Kristel Wills
Designed by Steve Potter and Jenica Wilkie

Printed in China

WORKING**TOGETHER**WORKS

BE A **GREAT PART**

You can go it alone if you want to, but life and work are a lot more fun, and far more productive, when we're pulling together as a winning team.

It's true. Everyone in a company or team should believe that he or she has something to give the organization which cannot otherwise be given. And, as Hugh Hanels puts it, "You make others better by being so good yourself."

How much better? That's the exciting part. Every day we see examples of teams or organizations that are obvious underdogs, but which are still out-playing, out-thinking and out-distancing their most formidable competitors. The lesson is simple and powerful, and can be found on virtually every page of "Team Works":

Great people don't necessarily equal great teams. A star team usually beats a team of stars. The best teams don't win nearly as often as the team that gets along best.

"Team Works" means intentionally and enthusiastically forming a band of winners that is greater that the sum of the individuals. The whole is the sum—and more—of its parts. So be a great part!

Dan Zadra

EXCELLENCE IS NOT A SPECTATOR SPORT. EVERYONE'S INVOLVED

—JACK WELCH

Great companies and great teams
set aside personal agendas to focus
all their resources on a common goal.
—A.L. SCHMITT

There is no such thing as an
individual sport nor a sole proprietorship.
There are a lot of people behind the
scenes for anything great to happen.
—KYLE DIERCKS

The major job was getting everyone
to understand that they had something
within their personal power that they
could use and contribute.
—ELLA BAKER

Who are the most important
people in the company? Everyone.
—PETE SELLECK

Everyone in a company or team
should believe that he or she has
something to give to the organization
which cannot otherwise be given.
—DAN ZADRA

8

Everyone has a unique role to fill.
Everyone, including and perhaps
especially you, is indispensable.
—NATHANIEL HAWTHORNE

TEAM

People are a firm's most important
asset. If you have an excellent product
but only mediocre people, the results
will only be mediocre.
—RICHARD SLOMA

People are not our most important asset.
The right people are.
—JIM COLLINS

You make others better by being
so good yourself.
—HUGH R. HANELS

WE ARE A WINNING
TEAM IN WHICH ALL
MEMBERS ARE VITAL.
WE PULL TOGETHER AS
ONE, LEARN FROM EACH
OTHER AND NEVER LET
A TEAMMATE FAIL.

—SUNSERVICE

The best thing about teamwork is
that you always have others on your side.
— MARGARET CARTY

The nice part about working with a
team of people is that when I don't know
what I'm doing, someone else does.
— KELLY ANN ROTHAUS

My weakness may be your strength,
and vice versa. When we work as a team,
the strengths cancel the weaknesses.
The result is mutual respect and
confidence throughout the entire team.
— MIKE POWER

Great people don't
necessarily equal great teams.
—TOM PETERS

Don't expect team players if you
haven't made it a team sport.
—BARRY MAHER

A star team usually beats
a team of stars.
—BEN WALLACE

TEAM

Draw strength from each other.
—JAMES A. RENIER

The best team doesn't win nearly as often
as the team that gets along best!
—DR. ROB GILBERT

A team can win with almost any offense,
provided everyone is playing the
same offense.
—JOHN WOODEN

13

ORKS

**TEAMWORK IS
LESS "EGO" AND
MORE "WE GO."**

—BRIAN BIRO

None of us is as smart as all of us.
— KEN BLANCHARD

Teamwork means never having to say,
"That's not my job." It means I'll be there
at any time you need my help, and I'll
do my best to help you do your job
in any way I can.
— JOHN ABLAKAT

You will find people who want to be
carried on the shoulders of others, who
think that the world owes them a living.
They don't seem to see that we must
lift together and pull together.
— HENRY FORD

Teamwork is forming a service
delivery "unit" that is stronger than
the sum of the individuals involved.
—DON FINCH

The whole is the sum of the parts.
Be a good part.
—NATE McCONNELL

Greatness is a perception. It may or
may not be reality. What is important is that
this reality is shared by many other people.
—CHARLOTTE CHANDLER

TEAM\

The main ingredient of stardom
is the rest of the team.
— JOHN WOODEN

A good objective of leadership is
to help those who are doing poorly
to do well and to help those who
are doing well to do even better.
— JIM ROHN

Put two people with a common
goal together and, suddenly,
one plus one is more than two.
— UNKNOWN

WHAT DRIVES THESE
PEOPLE IS NOT A
DESIRE FOR POWER
BUT A DESIRE TO HAVE
A POSITIVE INFLUENCE
ON THEIR WORKPLACE
AND THE WORLD.

—DARWIN SANOY

Today's employees are not just there for the money. They want meaningful work, they want to make a difference, and they want to feel like they belong.

— ROGER HERMAN

Work has to include our deepest values and passions and feelings and commitments, or it's not work, it's just a job.

— MATTHEW FOX

The people who are crazy enough to think they can change the world are the ones who do.

— APPLE COMPUTER, INC.

Is not life a hundred times too short
for us to bore ourselves?
— FRIEDRICH NIETZSCHE

All who have accomplished great things
have had a great aim, have fixed their
gaze on a goal which was high, one
which sometimes seemed impossible.
— ORISON SWETT MARDEN

20

We are called upon to become creators,
to make the world new and in that sense
to bring something into being which
was not there before.
— JOHN ELOF BOODIN

TEAM

Strategy is not something that's done in a box with only a rational hat on. It needs to be visceral, human, and often emotional— and everyone must be involved in creating it.

—ROBERT STONE

With our Core Values in place, making decisions is an easy process for me and my team. We know that any decision based on our values will be supported. These values empower us to be quick thinkers, and to move forward with high integrity and confidence.

—SHEILA O'BRIEN, SUN MICROSYSTEMS

WHAT DOES IT MEAN
TO BE PROMOTED INTO
A LEADERSHIP POSITION?
FRANKLY, IT MEANS NOW
WE HAVE THE AUTHORITY
TO SERVE PEOPLE IN
A SPECIAL WAY.

—ANONYMOUS

Very few natural-born leaders turn up
in the workplace. People become leaders.
— MILTON COTTER

Understanding that leaders come in
all flavors and sizes frees us to contemplate
our own eligibility for leadership roles.
— DAYLE M. SMITH

The times do not allow anyone the luxury of
waiting around for others to lead. All can
lead and ought to be invited to do so.
— MATTHEW FOX

23

We have no difficulty finding the leaders:
They have people following them.
—WILLIAM L. GORE

Those who enjoy responsibility
usually get it; those who merely like
exercising authority usually lose it.
—MALCOLM FORBES

True leadership is the art of changing a
group from what it is into what it ought
to be. It's not something that is done "to"
people, it is something done "with" people.
By that definition, every person
on the team is a leader.
—JAN GREENE

24

TEAM

Leadership is an attitude before
it becomes an ability.
—A.S. MIGS DAMIANI

Imagine if everyone in the company
had the courage and the confidence and
the risk-seeking profile that we associate
with leaders. That's the direction every
company must head.
—CHANCE DUNCAN

People willingly give you permission to
lead and influence them once they become
convinced how much you care for them.
—JACK LANNOM

OUR LUCK IS HOW WE TREAT PEOPLE.

—BRIDGET O'DONNELL

I believe the highest form of praise
you can give any individual is
sincere and simple respect.
—CAROL TRAMONTA

It's impossible to treat our customers
any better than we treat ourselves.
Great service starts on the inside of an
organization—with the way we treat
our co-workers and teammates—
and then works its way out.
—DAN ZADRA

People who matter most are most aware
that everyone else matters, too.
—MALCOLM FORBES

Good leaders let people know that
they're at the very heart of things, not at
the periphery. Everyone feels that he
or she makes a difference to the success
of the organization. When that happens
people feel centered and that gives
their work meaning.

— WARREN BENNIS

Great companies respect their customers
and employees—people at all levels and
from all backgrounds. By showing respect
for others, an organization or team itself
becomes respected. It rises in stature, and
makes a positive impact on the world.

— JAMES COLLINS

TEAM

Surround yourself with people who
respect you and treat you well.
—CLAUDIA BLACK

Right now it requires daily acts of heroism
for people to stand up and say what they
think the boss doesn't want to hear. It ought
to be good, clean give-and-take.
—SAM CULBERT

Really big people are, above
everything else, courteous, considerate, and
generous—not just to some people in some
circumstances—but to everyone all the time.
—THOMAS J. WATSON, JR.

WORKS

**THIS IS A
TEAM EFFORT.
IF YOU CAN'T PUT
PEOPLE UP, PLEASE
DON'T PUT THEM
DOWN.**

—NASA SLOGAN

It is easier to
pull down than to build up.
— FRANK VIZZARE

If you show people you don't care,
they'll return the favor.

— UNKNOWN

Help each other be right,
not wrong.
— IAN PERCY

More people get run down
by gossip than by cars.
— MARILYN WOLF

Gossip is a two-headed snake that poisons
everyone—the one who gossips, the one
who listens, and the one gossiped about.
— FRANK VIZZARE

32

Little people keep secrets.
Big people share ideas.
— PHIL ROGNIER

TEAM

It's not the critic who counts.
— THEODORE ROOSEVELT

Criticism should always leave people with
the feeling that they have been helped.
— UNKNOWN

When I must criticize somebody,
I do it orally; when I praise
somebody, I put it in writing.
— LEE IACOCCA

33

THERE ARE PEOPLE
WHO TAKE THE HEART
OUT OF YOU, AND
THERE ARE PEOPLE
WHO PUT IT BACK.

—ELIZABETH DAVID

The sweetest of all sounds
is sincere praise.
— XENOPHON

Appreciate people.
Nothing gives more joy.
— RUTH SMELTZER

The two kinds of people
on earth that I mean,
Are the people who lift
and the people who lean.
— ELLA WHEELER WILCOX

What you praise you increase.
— CATHERINE PONDER

There must've been hundreds of people
cheering at some of those track meets,
but my father's voice always found me.
A simple, "That's it kid," and my
feet grew wings.
— MADISON RILEY

Look, when that crowd gets to cheering,
when we know they're with us, when
we know they like us, we play better.
A heck of a lot better!
— BILL CARLINE

TEAM

To keep that good feeling
you get from a sincere compliment,
pay one to someone else.
— DON WARD

If you look for the good in others,
you'll discover the best in yourself.
— BOB MOAWAD

The key is to keep company with
people who uplift you, whose
presence calls forth your best.
— EPICTETUS

EVERYONE WHO DOES THE BEST HE OR SHE CAN DO SHOULD BE CONSIDERED A HERO.

—JOSH BILLINGS

When people act heroically,
treat them as heroes.
— JEFF GOFORTH

People work for self-expression.
Even when they talk loudest about "getting
the money" they are really most interested
in doing a job skillfully, and getting that
inward glow which comes of achievement.
— HOWARD V. O'BRIEN

When someone does
something good, applaud!
You will make two people happy.
— SAMUEL GOLDWYN

People are in greater need of
your praise when they try and fail,
than when they try and succeed.
—BOB MOAWAD

The only thing that keeps us from
floating off with the wind is our stories.
They give us a name and put us in a place,
allow us to keep on touching.
—TOM SPANBAUER

People come together because they
need each other and they need to hear
victories about each other.
—BILL MILLIKEN

TEAM

People must believe in each other, and
feel that it can be done and must be done;
in that way they are enormously strong.
—VINCENT VAN GOGH

Appreciation is like an insurance policy.
It has to be renewed every now and then.
—DAVE McINTRYRE

People often say that motivation doesn't last.
Well, neither does bathing—that's why we
recommend it daily.
—ZIG ZIGLAR

WHEN YOU HANDLE YOURSELF, USE YOUR HEAD; WHEN YOU HANDLE OTHERS, USE YOUR HEART.

—DONNA REED

Hidden agendas destroy trust.
—JUDITH M. BARDWICK

Keeping close to the vest, going around
people and hiding things is behavior
from the last century. Creating an "open"
environment will bring solutions we never
dreamed of.
—TOM PICKETT

43

The trick is to get people communicating
on a personal level. Who knows, we
might even end up liking each other.
—DANETT LEE

If you can't say it to everybody,
don't say it to anybody.
—JANICE LAROUCHE AND REGINA RYAN

Be loyal to people in their absence.
—STEPHEN COVEY

44

We are all bruised, so let's eliminate
life's little irritations for each other.
The motto should be, "Let's reduce
friction to a fraction."
—GUY CLARKE

TEAM

Everyone has in them
something precious that is in no one else.
—MARTIN BUBER

Take your heart to work and ask the
most and best of yourself and everybody
else. Don't let your special character
and spirit—the true essence of you—
don't let that get beaten down.
—MERYL STREEP

A great coach doesn't try to change a great
player. Instead, the coach discovers what is
unique, what is great, about people
and honors it, is happy for it, uses it.
—JOHN BUNN

WORKS

WHEN BUILDING A TEAM,
I ALWAYS SEARCH FOR
PEOPLE WHO LOVE TO WIN.
IF I CAN'T FIND ANY OF
THOSE, I LOOK FOR PEOPLE
WHO HATE TO LOSE.

—ROSS PEROT

You have to build an organization of people who are not only capable, but also hungry.
— JASON ELSMORE

When people say they are committed, they don't say that we "hope" to win, or it would sure be "nice" to win, or we "wouldn't mind" winning. They say, and they mean, that they are committed to winning.
— DON WARD

Every time you win, you're reborn.
— GEORGE ALLEN

The more difficult a victory,
the greater the happiness in winning.
—PELE

Winning is important to me, but what brings
me real joy is the experience of being fully
engaged in whatever I'm doing.
—PHIL JACKSON

The most important lesson you can learn
from winning is that you can.
—DAVE WEINBAUM

TEAM\

The wonderful thing about the
game of life is that winning and losing
are only temporary—unless you quit.
—DR. FRED MILLS

The difference between winning
and losing is frequently not quitting.
—WALT DISNEY

Ninety percent of those who fail are not
actually defeated. They simply quit.
—PAUL J. MEYER

The tragedy of life is not that
we lose, but that we almost win.
— HEYWOOD BROWN

Most people give up just when
they're about to achieve success.
They quit on the one yard line.
They give up the last minute of the game
one foot from a winning touchdown.
— ROSS PEROT

It's hard to beat a team that never gives up.
— BABE RUTH

50

TEAM

If you keep working at it, in the
last analysis you win. They've got
to kill us a hundred times. All we
have to do is kill them once.

—FRED SMITH

We are not interested in the
possibilities of defeat.

—QUEEN VICTORIA

Ride on over all obstacles,
and win the race.

—CHARLES DICKENS

**THOSE ON TOP
OF THE MOUNTAIN
DIDN'T FALL THERE.**

—GIL ATKINSON

Winners are known as much
by the quality of their failures as by
the quality of their successes.
— MARK McCORMACK, IMG

I have missed more than 9,000 shots in
my career. I have lost almost 300 games.
On 26 occasions I have been entrusted to
take the game winning shot...and missed.
I have failed over and over again in my life.
And that is why I succeed.
— MICHAEL JORDAN

53

I don't think anything is unrealistic if
you believe you can do it.
— MIKE DITKA

Being challenged in life is
inevitable, being defeated is optional.
—ROGER CRAWFORD

Champions keep playing
until they get it right.
—BILLIE JEAN KING

Obstacles don't make people stop—
people stop themselves.
—CAROL QUINN

TEAM\

Ignore people who say it can't be done.
— ELAINE RIDEOUT

Vince Lombardi didn't become a
head coach in the NFL until he was 47.
Eddie Arcaro lost his first 45 races.
Michael Jordan was cut from his high
school basketball team. It's not how
you start, it's how you finish.
— DAN ZADRA

Defeat is not the worst of failures.
Not to have tried is the true failure.
— GEORGE E. WOODBERRY

WORKS

SO CELEBRATE WHAT
YOU'VE ACCOMPLISHED,
BUT RAISE THE BAR
A LITTLE HIGHER EACH
TIME YOU SUCCEED.

—MIA HAMM

Talent is never enough.
With a few exceptions, the best
players are the hardest workers.
—EARVIN "MAGIC" JOHNSON

You can't cut corners if you want
to be great. Natural skills are fine,
but work makes you a champion.
—BEN WALLACE

Anybody with guts and the desire to
apply himself can make it, he can make
anything he wants to make of himself.
—WILLIE SHOEMAKER

The toughest competition comes from
the rival you've never heard of—and if
you don't think there are rivals out there,
you're kidding yourself.

—ROBERT LITAN

Have you learned lessons only of those
who admired you, and were tender with you,
and stood aside for you? Have you
not learned great lessons from those who
braced themselves against you, and
disputed the passage with you?

—WALT WHITMAN

No matter what the competition is, I try to
find a goal that day and better that goal.

—BONNIE BLAIR

TEAM

I've always had something to shoot for
each year: to jump one inch farther.
—JACKIE JOYNER-KERSEE, OLYMPIC LONG JUMPER

Try that new little thing, that different
approach. Get out of your comfort zone
and see if it works.
—MARY LOU RETTON

59

Winning doesn't always mean being first.
Winning means you're doing better than
you've ever done before.
—BONNIE BLAIR

To build a good team make sure everyone
can give and receive criticism. I know I am
not the perfect player or person, so I'm always
open to what my teammates have to say,
positive or negative. If I can get better,
it will only help the team.

— BEN WALLACE

The answers to three questions will
determine your success or failure:
1. Can people trust me to do my best?
2. Am I committed to the task at hand?
3. Do I care about other people and show it?
If the answers to these questions are yes,
there is no way you can fail.

— LOU HOLTZ

TEAM

There are plenty of teams in every sport
that have great players and never win
titles. Most of the time, those players aren't
willing to sacrifice for the greater good of
the team. The funny thing is, in the end,
their unwillingness to sacrifice only makes
individual goals more difficult to achieve.
One thing I believe to the fullest is that if you
think and achieve as a team, the individual
accolades will take care of themselves.
Talent wins games, but teamwork and
intelligence win championships.

—MICHAEL JORDAN

DON'T BELIEVE THAT WINNING IS REALLY EVERYTHING. IT'S MORE IMPORTANT TO STAND FOR SOMETHING. IF YOU DON'T STAND FOR SOMETHING, WHAT DO YOU WIN?

—JOSEPH LANE KIRKLAND

We all need to believe
in what we're doing.
— ALLAN GILMOUR

If people believe in the
company they work for, they
pour their hearts into
making it better.
— HOWARD SCHULTZ, STARBUCKS

A company finds its destiny by
answering three questions:
Who are we? What do we stand for?
How do we serve?
— TOM CHAPPELL

It isn't common ground that bonds
people together, it's higher ground.
—TOM BROWN

Just getting people in the same
place at the same time does not
produce a team. Community requires
a common vision and shared values.
—DIANE DREHER

Leaders and followers are both
following the invisible leader—the big
idea—their shared purpose and values.
—DAN ZADRA

TEAM

Organizations exist only for one purpose:
To help people reach ends together that
they couldn't achieve individually.
—ROBERT H. WATERMAN

People are saying, "I want a company and
a job that values me as much as I value it.
I want something in my life not just to invest
my time in, but to believe in."
—ANITA RODDICK

People will work eight hours a day for pay,
10 hours a day for a good boss, and 24
hours a day for a good cause!
—JOHN C. MAXWELL

YE GADS, WAKE
UP! BREATHE! GO
DOWN SWINGING.
TRY SOMETHING. TRY
ANYTHING. BE A-L-I-V-E,
FOR HEAVEN'S SAKE!

—TOM PETERS

We run this business with our hearts—
and we show it every chance we get.
It's not our culture to be complacent.
—NORMAN MAYNE

There must be bands of enthusiasts for
everything on earth—fanatics who share
a vocabulary, a batch of technical skills
and equipment, and perhaps, a vision of
some single slice of the beauty and mystery
of things, of their complexity, fascination,
and unexpectedness.
—ANNIE DILLARD

The world is moved by highly
motivated people, by enthusiasts, by
men and women who want something
very much or believe very much.

—JOHN GARDNER

Purpose is the engine that fires
your dream and your team.

—DR. ROBERT SCHULLER

There is one thing we can do, and
the best people and the best companies
do this. We can be completely present.
We can give all our attention to the
opportunity before us.

—MARK VAN DOREN

TEAM

Caring is a powerful business advantage.
—SCOTT JOHNSON

The one piece of advice which will
contribute to making you a better leader,
will provide you with greater happiness
and will advance your career more than
any other advice—and it doesn't call
for a special personality or any certain
chemistry—and any one of you can do it.
And that advice is: You must care.
—LT. GENERAL MELVIN ZAIS

WE CAN'T SWEEP
OUR CUSTOMERS
OFF THEIR FEET, IF
WE CAN'T BE SWEPT
OFF OUR OWN.

—JAMES EARLY

Passion. Creativity. Commitment. ·
Those are the qualities that companies
need most if they want to win in the new
world of business. Those are also the
qualities that are lacking at most companies.
— JIM STUART

If you love what you do, and you feel
that it matters, then the passion will show.
In today's world, "I care" is not just a
nice phrase: it's a two-word recipe for
excellence, success and fulfillment.
— UNKNOWN

I can accept failure. Everyone fails at
something. But I can't accept not trying.
— MICHAEL JORDAN

Commitment is what moves a
group to become a team.
— DAVID QUINLIVAN-HALL

From my experience, great companies,
great cities, great football teams and
Nobel-winning efforts are all unfailingly led
by people with a consuming passion for
their discipline, product and customer.
— TOM PETERS

TEAM

People say don't take business personally—
but that's my work, my sweat, my time away
from my family. How can that not be personal?
— ELAINE BRANSON

I won't accept anything less than the
best a player's capable of doing and he
has the right to expect the best that
I can do for him and the team!
— LOU HOLTZ

Don't work for my happiness, my brothers—
show me yours. Show me that it's possible—
show me your achievement—and the
knowledge will give me courage for mine.
— AYN RAND, "THE FOUNTAINHEAD"

WORKS

**ENTHUSIASM IS
CONTAGIOUS.
BE A CARRIER.**

—SUSAN RABIN

Notice that the most interesting,
charismatic people are virtually
always talking about what they are for,
rather than what they are against.

— UNKNOWN

Some people have thousands of
reasons why they cannot do what
they want to, when all they need is
one reason why they can.

— MARY FRANCES BERRY

Somebody is always doing what somebody
else said couldn't be done.

— UNKNOWN

Watch what people are cynical about, and
one can often discover what they lack.
—GENERAL GEORGE S. PATTON

There's a very thin line between
successful people and unsuccessful ones.
Crossing over to the successful side requires
only a subtle evolution in mindset.
—GARY GABEL

We either make ourselves miserable
or we make ourselves strong.
The amount of work is same.
—CARLOS CASTANEDA

TEAM

There is little difference in people, but
that little difference makes a big difference.
That little difference is attitude. The big
difference is whether it is positive or negative.
— W. CLEMENT STONE

There is nothing as easy as denouncing.
It don't take much to see that something is
wrong, but it takes some eyesight to see
what will put it right again.
— WILL ROGERS

The real winners in life look at every
situation with an expectation that they
can make it work or make it better.
— BARBARA PLETCHER

WORKS

**REMEMBER THAT
20 PERCENT OF
THE PEOPLE ARE
AGAINST EVERYTHING
ALL THE TIME.**

—ROBERT F. KENNEDY

Some people seem to go through life
standing at the complaint counter.
— FRED PROPP, JR.

Some people miss the message because
they are too busy checking the spelling.
— MAYNARD C. CARNEY

An optimist stays up until midnight to see
the new year in. A pessimist stays up
to make sure the old year leaves.
— BILL VAUGHAN

If the answer is no, you have asked
the wrong person.
—RONI MILES

Believe that problems do have answers,
that they can be overcome, and
that you can solve them.
—NORMAN VINCENT PEALE

Pessimists calculate the odds. Optimists
believe they can overcome them.
—TED KOPPEL

TEAM

Those who do not
hope to win have already lost.
— JOAQUIN OLMEDOE

People who only come up with
"It may not work" or "What are we
going to do if it fails?" do not have
the credentials to be businessmen.
— KIM WOO-CHOONG,
FOUNDER AND CHAIRMAN, DAEWOO

When people tell you, "No," just smile
and tell them, "Yes, I can."
— JULIE FOUDY

STRONG CORPORATE
CULTURES COME FROM
WITHIN, AND THEY ARE
BUILT BY EVERY PERSON
INSIDE THE COMPANY.

—CRAIG R. HICKMAN

So much of excellence in performance
has to do with people being motivated by
compelling, simple—even beautiful—values.
These shared values create a broad,
uplifting culture—a coherent framework—
within which charged-up people search for
appropriate ways to make extraordinary
contributions to the overall higher purpose.

—TOM PETERS

The trouble is that not enough people have come together with the firm determination to live the things which they say they believe in.
— ELEANOR ROOSEVELT

Lots of companies have their Vision, Mission and Values on the wall. How many have them in their minds and hearts?
— DAN ZADRA

Success is seizing the day and accepting responsibility for your future. It's seeing what other people don't see, and pursuing that vision, no matter who tells you not to.
— HOWARD SCHULTZ, STARBUCKS

TEAM\

Superior work teams recognize that
consistently high performance can be
built not on rules, but only on values.
—DENNIS KINLAW

The best reason to commit half your waking
hours to a company or organization is because
a large group of like-minded people can
usually accomplish something bigger and
more satisfying than they could alone.
—DAN ZADRA

Successful teams are just ordinary folks
who have developed a belief in
each other and what they do.
—DAVID SCHWARTZ

ORKS

TEAM SPIRIT—CONSIDERATION FOR OTHERS—IS THE GREAT HOPE FOR US ALL.

—BRIAN BIRO

The way to develop the
best that is in an individual or a team
is by appreciation and encouragement.
—CHARLES SCHWAB

Encouragement is oxygen to the soul.
—UNKNOWN

Note how good you feel after you have
encouraged someone else. No other
argument is necessary to suggest that
one should never miss the opportunity
to give encouragement.
—GEORGE ADAMS

To believe in someone is
the greatest gift that you can give.
—TERRE JASPER

You can work miracles by having
faith in others. To inspire the best
in people, choose to think and
believe the best about them.

—BOB MOAWAD

Treat people as if they were what they ought
to be, and you help them to become what
they are capable of becoming.
—JOHANN VON GOETHE

TEAM

If the people around you don't believe
in you, if they don't encourage you, then
you need to find some people who do.
—JOHN MAXWELL

Those who believe in our ability
do more than stimulate us: They
create for us an atmosphere in which
it becomes easier to succeed.
—JOHN H. SPALDING

People become really quite remarkable
when they start thinking that they can do
things. When they believe in themselves
they have the first secret of success.
—NORMAN VINCENT PEALE

THOSE WITH WHOM WE WORK LOOK TO US FOR HEAT AS WELL AS LIGHT.

—WOODROW WILSON

In order to burn out, a person needs
to have been on fire at one time.
—AYALA PINES

It's hard for me to keep my
emotions inside. I want to express them
now. That's what a team is all about.
—EARVIN "MAGIC" JOHNSON

Dedication to excellence on any level,
in any area, requires an intensity of
emotional investment. Unfortunately,
there are scores of people who do not
make the investment—who do not
feel strongly about anything.
—THEODORE ISAAC RUBIN

The people I have found to be
most successful are not necessarily
the smartest people, but the people
with the most spirit and enthusiasm.

—DONALD TRUMP

The success or failure of any company boils
down to one question: Are you operating
from passion? If you are, you're going
to succeed. If you believe in what you're
doing, you're going to make sure that
everyone around you believes in it too.

—MAGGIE HUGHES

TEAM

It's important to take pride in what
you do or what you stand for. The kind
of pride I'm talking about is not the
arrogant puffed-up kind; it's just the
whole idea of caring—fiercely caring.
—RED AUERBACH

Walking up and down the halls I feel at
home with my company. Everyone is treated
the same and teamwork is highly emphasized.
I am proud to tell people where I work.
—ERIC WEST

Enthusiasm begets enthusiasm.
—HENRY WADSWORTH LONGFELLOW

MY IDEA OF A
SUCCESSFUL MEETING
IS WHEN SOMEBODY
ATTENDS AND SAYS,
"I COULDN'T TELL WHO
WORKED FOR WHOM."

—CHUCK BEYER

If he works for you, you work for him.
— JAPANESE PROVERB

The best leader does not ask people to
serve him, but the common end. The best
leader has not followers, but men and
women working with him.

95

— MARY PARKER FOLLETT

If you honor and serve the people who work
for you, they will honor and serve you.
— MARY KAY ASH

The joy of leadership is helping others succeed.
—GALE SMITH

The function of leadership is to produce more leaders, not more followers.
—RALPH NADER

Creating a leadership mindset throughout the organization begins with setting the expectation that each individual is a leader.
—GAYLE LANTZ

TEAM

Hire good people and let them be good.
—CLAY RAMSEY

Few things can help an individual more than
to place responsibility on him, and to let him
know that you trust him.
—BOOKER T. WASHINGTON

Good leaders inspire people to have
confidence in them. Great leaders inspire
people to have confidence in themselves.
—SAM EWING

LET PEOPLE ACCOMPLISH YOUR OBJECTIVES THEIR WAY.

—CLARK JOHNSON

Never tell people how to do things.
Tell them what to do and they will
surprise you with ingenuity.
—GENERAL GEORGE S. PATTON

The best way to make people
trustworthy is to trust them.
—ANONYMOUS

The best leaders will be those who
listen to their people to figure out
where they should be going.
—JACK KAHL

Powerful people are seen as such
because they have the capacity to give
power to others and they do so.
—ROBIN BOWMAN

When you give people power, you give
them strength to make you strong.
—EVELYN DUNN

100

Leadership is different than management.
Management is about what you can control.
Leadership is about what you can unleash.
—DAN ZADRA

TEAM

The job of the leader is not
to kick people in the butt.
—UNKNOWN

Managers light a fire under people;
leaders light a fire in people.
—KATHY AUSTIN

If your actions inspire others to dream more,
learn more, do more, and become more,
you are a leader.
—JOHN QUINCY ADAMS

101

DONUTS: THE ONLY NON-NEGOTIABLE ELEMENT TO A SUCCESSFUL MEETING.

—JOE HEUER

Courage is what it takes to
stand up and speak; courage is also
what it takes to sit down and listen.
—WINSTON CHURCHILL

Listening: You can convey no
greater honor than actually hearing
what someone has to say.
—"QUALITY IS FREE"

Listening is about trust and respect and
involvement and information sharing
more than it is about ears.
—BEVERLY BRIGGS, "CUSTOMER CONNECTION NEWSLETTER"

Arguments begin when listening stops.
—UNKNOWN

All of us need to lower our
voices. All of us need to look
at our common purposes.
—DONNA SHALALA

Do not condemn the judgment of
another because it differs from your own.
You may both be wrong.
—DANDEMIS

TEAM

Great evil has been done on earth by
people who think they have all the answers.
— RUBY PLENTY CHIEFS

People who think they know everything are
a great annoyance to those of us who do.
— ANONYMOUS

It's easier for people to see it your way if
you first see it their way.
— JACK KAINE

IF COMMUNICATION IS NOT YOUR TOP PRIORITY, ALL OF YOUR OTHER PRIORITIES ARE AT RISK.

—BOB ARONSON

Communication is the essential
life blood of organizational life.
— ANN HARRIMAN

If we have honest conversations
about what's working and what isn't,
we can become really good. If we don't,
we never really help each other.
— DAVE BARRAM

107

Before you speak, ask yourself if what
you are going to say is true, is kind, is
necessary, is helpful. If the answer is no,
maybe what you are about to say
should be left unsaid.
— BERNARD MELTZER

You need a team environment that clearly
conveys this dominant message to everyone:
"If you have a problem, you need to bring
it up because we'll listen."

—STEPHEN PASKOFF

Listening with empathy requires patience,
trust, openness, and, above all,
a desire to understand.

—STEVEN SAINT AND JAMES R. LAWSON

"How can I help you?" is a question we
ask our customers every day. I believe it's
a question we should be asking our co-
workers and teammates every day, as well.

—RON KENDRICK

TEAM

Make sure everybody's onboard the train.
— MIKE KRZYZEWSKI

One of the greatest misconceptions
that people live in is that they don't
make a difference.
— MARTHA LOUIS

Wise leaders know that if an individual   109
doesn't count, the institution doesn't count
for much either. Put mathematically, if the
individual is a zero, together a lot of zeros
add up to a whole lot of nothing.
— DIANE DREHER

VORKS

FOSTER THE ATTITUDE, "LET'S FIX THE PROBLEM, NOT PLACE THE BLAME."

—"BUILDING COMMUNITY"

The search for someone to blame
is always successful.
—ROBERT HALF

Recently, I was asked if I was going
to fire an employee who made a
mistake that cost the company $600,000.
No, I replied, I just spent $600,000
training him. Why would I want
somebody to hire his experience?
—THOMAS J. WATSON, JR.

111

Nobody stands taller than those willing
to stand corrected.
—WILLIAM SAFIRE

You win some and you learn some.
— BARRY JOHNSON

The next best thing to winning is losing!
At least you've been in the race.
— NELLIE HERSHEY SMITH

Sometimes you have to lose major
championships before you can win them.
Losing is a learning experience that's
worth a fortune.
— TOM WATSON

TEAM

Problems can become opportunities when
the right people come together.
— ROBERT REDFORD

We can always depend on some
people to make the best, instead of
the worst, of whatever happens.
— SANDRA WILDE

You really don't know what your true
potential is until you've pushed yourself
beyond your limits. You have to fail
a couple of times to really find out
how far you can go.
— DEBI THOMAS

ORKS

IF WE'RE NOT BIG ENOUGH TO LOSE, WE'RE NOT BIG ENOUGH TO WIN.

—WALTER REUTHER

No one can become a winner without
losing many, many times.
—MARIE LINDQUIST

Fail forward! Whenever you undertake
a new project, attempt to make as many
mistakes as rapidly as possible in order to
learn as much as you can in the shortest
period of time. Mistakes are great.
Learn from them, research them,
use them to propel you forward.
—UNKNOWN

Make it a safe environment for people
around you. Allow them the opportunity
to make and learn from their mistakes.
—UNKNOWN

You've got to have an atmosphere
where people can make mistakes.
If we're not making mistakes,
we're not going anywhere.
—GORDON FORWARD

To swear off making mistakes is very easy.
All we have to do is swear off having ideas.
—LEO BURNETT

TEAM

The only people who never fail
are those who never try.
—ILKA CHASE

People who don't take risks generally
make about two big mistakes a year.
People who do take risks generally make
about two big mistakes a year.
—PETER DRUCKER

You're going to make mistakes in life.
It's what you do after them that counts.
—BRANDI CHASTAIN

VORKS

A BALANCED LIFE—
I'VE HEARD OF IT!

—LES KURTZ

Out of chaos comes the dance of balance.
—DENISE KESTER

In our company we move heaven and earth
to help each other balance our lives.
—MICHAEL NOLAN

We all have people on our teams who are
notorious overachievers. Let's be involved
enough in the activity of the people who
report to us so we know when to help
them go home to their families!
—JOHN DRISCOLL

You live longer once you realize that any
time spent being unhappy is wasted.
—RUTH E. RENKL

Work and play are the same. When you're
following your energy and doing what you
want all the time, the distinction between
work and play dissolves.
—SHAKTI GAWAIN

120

Whether you are burning midnight oil
on a project or celebrating a win, "fun"
is a combination of enjoying what you
do and with whom you do it.
—MIKE SINGLETON

TEAM

Serious people have few ideas.
People with ideas are never serious.
— PAUL VALERY

People are going to be most creative
and productive when they're doing
something they're really interested in.
So having fun isn't an outrageous idea
at all. It's a very sensible one.
— JOHN SCULLEY

Just play. Have fun. Enjoy the game.
— MICHAEL JORDAN

SOMETIMES, I THINK
THE THINGS WE SEE
ARE SHADOWS OF
THE THINGS TO BE;
THAT WHAT WE PLAN
WE BUILD...

—PHOEBE CARY

Exploration is really the
essence of the human spirit.
—FRANK BORMAN

Change is a door that can
only be opened from the inside.
—TERRY NEILL

For changes to occur, you have to
embrace them over and over. Take it
step by step—but keep moving forward—
and a year from now, you'll find you've
moved from here to there.
—RHONDA ABRAMS

The future is not someplace we are going to, but a place we are creating. The paths to it are not found, they are made.
— JANE GARVEY

Should-haves solve nothing. It's the next thing to happen that needs thinking about.
— ALEXANDRA RIPLEY

Smart organizations of the future won't try to manage change processes. Instead they will nurture the spirit of change within their people. That way, change will occur naturally, and it will preserve the heart and soul of the organization.
— SUE SIMMONS

Send a clear message to every
member of your team that your company
stands for something wonderful—that its
Mission in the world is valuable, worthwhile
and important—that it brings value to lives.
Let them know over and over again that the
work they do each day contributes directly
to the Mission, and really does make a
difference. Engage with team members on
a personal level. Listen closely to their
dreams, hopes, plans and ideas. Challenge
them to grow and excel, and then recognize
and celebrate them when they do.

—DAN ZADRA

WORKS

There can be no progress
unless people have faith in tomorrow.
—JOHN F. KENNEDY

We must give up the way it is
in order to have it the way we want it.
—UNKNOWN

Today is your day and mine, the only day
we have, the day in which we play our
part—and the whole world is starting to
feel it all at once. It is no time for cynicism.
This is our time to grow and build and love.
—ELIE SHULMAN

LET EACH OF US WORK
TO BUILD ORGANIZATIONS
WHERE EVERYONE CAN MAKE
A CONTRIBUTION—WHERE
EVERYBODY COUNTS—
ORGANIZATIONS WHICH
WILL CONTINUE TO
CHANGE THE WORLD.

—ELIZABETH DOLE

Other "Gift of Inspiration" books available:

Be Happy
**Remember to live, love,
laugh and learn**

Be the Difference

Because of You
Celebrating the Difference You Make

Brilliance
**Uncommon voices from
uncommon women**

Commitment to Excellence
Celebrating the Very Best

Diversity
Celebrating the Differences

Everyone Leads
**It takes each of us to make
a difference for all of us**

Expect Success
Our Commitment to Our Customer

Forever Remembered
A Gift for the Grieving Heart

I Believe in You
**To your heart, your dream, and the
difference you make**

Little Miracles
**Cherished messages of hope, joy,
love, kindness and courage**

Reach for the Stars
Give up the good to go for the great

Thank You
**In appreciation of you, and
all that you do**

To Your Success
**Thoughts to Give Wings to
Your Work and Your Dreams**

Together We Can
**Celebrating the power of a
team and a dream**

Welcome Home
Celebrating the Best Place on Earth

What's Next
Creating the Future Now

Whatever It Takes
**A Journey into the Heart
of Human Achievement**

You've Got a Friend
**Thoughts to Celebrate the
Joy of Friendship**

100530